WOULD YOU RATHER GAME BOOK FOR KIDS

GROSS EDITION

Cooper the Pooper

TABLE OF CONTENTS

INTRODUCTION

Have you ever wondered what would be worse? Being covered in cockroaches, or being covered in ants? Or what would be better? Smelling like dog poop, or having the smell of dog poop stuck in your nose forever?

What about being forced to eat bugs, or being eaten by bugs?

Now, I know what you are thinking – gross, right?
But still a little funny...

OK, very funny.
It does not stop there, because I have given you the chance to wonder about all sorts of gross things and have a big laugh in the process. See, in your hand you hold one of my favorite books that has 200 "would you rather" questions.

But not just any old questions.
In this book you will finds some of the grossest, most disgusting, most thought-provoking questions on the planet.

These questions will have you screwing up your face in shock. They will have you clutching your sides in laughter. And they will have you so confused that you will not know whether to giggle, cry, or scream from frustration.

Now I know what you are thinking – why in the world would a dog write a book?

Not so long ago I was a very normal dog. I spent my days chasing cats, digging holes, and running around with the neighborhood kids.

But then something happened – something bad.
Instead of play with me, the neighborhood kids began spending all their time inside playing video games.

Talk about boring.
And I started thinking of some ways kids just like you can have fun with your friends and family – which is why I decided to start writing books.

But not normal books.
Books that get you laughing. Books that get you thinking.
Books that you can share with your friends and family.
Books full to the brim with gross "would you rather" questions, for example…

So, what in the world are you waiting for? Hurry up and start laughing with your friends and family.

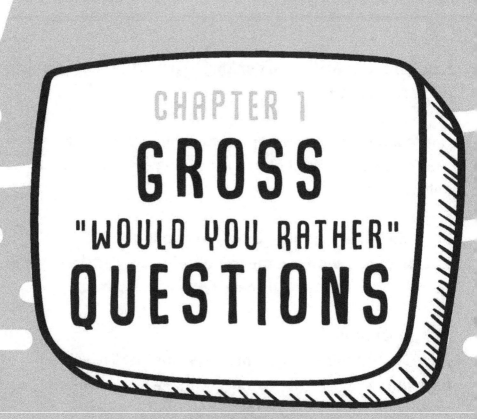

CHAPTER 1

GROSS
"WOULD YOU RATHER"
QUESTIONS

WOULD YOU RATHER...

01 Eat a cricket sandwich every day,

- OR -

Eat a mud brownie every day?

02 Eat earthworm spaghetti,

- OR -

Cockroach meatballs?

WOULD YOU RATHER...

03

Drink juice that smells like pee,

- OR -

Tea that tastes like moldy cheese?

04

Drink a cheese smoothie,

- OR -

A smoothie that tastes like toothpaste?

WOULD YOU RATHER...

05 wipe your friend's butt after they use the toilet,

- OR -

Pick their nose?

06 have someone spit in your mouth,

- OR -

In your eyeball?

WOULD YOU RATHER...

07

Wash your hands
with rotten milk,

- OR -

Have rotten eggs
massaged onto your back?

08

Sleep in a bed made
from human hair,

- OR -

One made from dog fur?

WOULD YOU RATHER...

09

Drink a glass of chunky, sour milk,

- OR -

Eat a rotten meat sandwich?

10

The air around you permanently smelling like farts,

- OR -

Like a tuna and egg salad?

WOULD YOU RATHER...

Have your food sprinkled with dandruff for an entire day,

- OR -

Sprinkled with fingernail clippings?

11

12

Eat a cookie made with rabbit droppings,

- OR -

One made with dead skin?

WOULD YOU RATHER...

13 Clean up your friend's vomit,

- OR -

Vomit uncontrollably for an entire day?

14 Rather eat a slimy slug,

- OR -

A really crunchy beetle?

WOULD YOU RATHER...

15

Bathe in a tub of syrup

- OR -

A tub of mud?

16

Have to eat like a pig,

- OR -

Like a shark for a month?

WOULD YOU RATHER...

17

Rather have to eat an entire chili,

- OR -

an entire lemon?

18

Drink a sardine smoothie,

- OR -

Grass-flavored ice cream sprinkled with crickets?

WOULD YOU RATHER...

19

Pick your friend's nose,

- OR -

Have them lick your face?

20

Eat noodles made from hair,

- OR -

Drink a glass of sweat?

WOULD YOU RATHER...

21

Have a huge boil on your bum,

- OR -

on your face?

22

Sweat continuously for
a whole day,

- OR -

Spend the whole day with
a leaky nose?

WOULD YOU RATHER...

23

Pop a huge pimple
on your friend's back,

- OR -

Have one grow on your chin?

24

Lick a pile of sand,

- OR -

Cover your body in mud?

WOULD YOU RATHER...

25

Drink dirty water,

- OR -

Eat food from the floor for the entire day?

26

Eat a sandwich that a stranger spat on,

- OR -

One that your friend sneezed on?

WOULD YOU RATHER...

27

Eat a piece of rotten meat

- OR -

a piece of raw meat?

28 Drink a glass of milk that tastes fine but smells like it has gone sour,

- OR -

Drink a glass of milk that smells fine but tastes like it has gone sour?

WOULD YOU RATHER...

29

Eat a cake made from broccoli,

- OR -

A pizza made from brussel sprouts?

30

Eat a cockroach covered in chocolate,

- OR -

a piece of chocolate covered in cockroaches?

WOULD YOU RATHER...

31

Eat a dead beetle,

- OR -

A live worm?

32 swim in a pool filled with chocolate pudding that tastes like mud,

- OR -

in a pool filled with mud that tastes like chocolate pudding?

WOULD YOU RATHER...

33

Sneeze out peanut butter,

- OR -

Cry chocolate sauce?

34

Eat a can of dog food,

- OR -

eat birdseed?

WOULD YOU RATHER...

35 Eat liver every day for lunch,

- OR -

Or sardines every day for breakfast?

36 Only eat and drink things that have gone rotten for a week,

- OR -

lick the floor before you eat anything?

WOULD YOU RATHER...

37

Eat an onion every day,

- OR -

Smell like an onion?

38 Permanently have a string of snot hanging out of your nose,

- OR -

Sneeze out a booger the size of a marble every time you sneeze?

WOULD YOU RATHER...

39

Have burps that smell like feet,

- OR -

Burps that taste like rotten eggs?

40

Have googly eyes that stared at everyone,

- OR -

A huge tongue that licked everyone that walked by?

WOULD YOU RATHER...

41

Have spaghetti for hair,

- OR -

Meatballs for eyes?

42

Only bathe once a month

- OR -

Sweat every time you step outside?

WOULD YOU RATHER...

43

Lick your friend's foot once,

- OR -

Have your friend put their foot on your face for an hour?

44

Poop out candy drops,

- OR -

Pee soda pop?

WOULD YOU RATHER...

45

Fingernails made of old chewed up bubblegum,

- OR -

Toenails made out of watermelon seeds?

46

Have your ears stuffed with boogers,

- OR -

Your nose stuffed with earwax?

WOULD YOU RATHER...

47

Burp uncontrollably every time you see food,

- OR -

Giggle every time you put something into your mouth?

48

Eat a plate of frog legs

- OR -

A bowl of pig feet?

WOULD YOU RATHER...

49

Eat a sardine sandwich,

- OR -

A liver burger every day
for lunch?

50

Sneeze out green snot,

- OR -

Sweat out blue sweat?

WOULD YOU RATHER...

51 Have a huge itchy rash on your butt,

- OR -

One on your hands?breakfast?

52 Touch your sibling's eyeball,

- OR -

Have them touch your eyeball?

WOULD YOU RATHER...

53
Have skin made from ham,

- OR -

Teeth made from little blocks of cheese?

54
Have feet for hands,

- OR -

Hands for feet?

WOULD YOU RATHER...

55

Have a really big tongue,

- OR -

Uncontrollably lick everyone you see?

56

Have the teeth of a walrus,

- OR -

Smell like a walrus?

WOULD YOU RATHER...

57

Have the body of a slug,

- OR -

Have to eat a slug?

58

Have a giant wart
on your bum,

- OR -

Have your head turn into a
giant wart?

WOULD YOU RATHER...

59 Fish fins in place of your real fingers,

- OR -

Have your hands always smelling like rotten fish?

60 Lick the inside of a trash can,

- OR -

The inside of a city bus?

WOULD YOU RATHER...

61

Smell a sewer every time you wake up,

- OR -

Smell a skunk every time you go to bed?

62

Vomit every time you see food,

- OR -

Have all of your food smell like vomit?

WOULD YOU RATHER...

63

Have your face be replaced by a giant foot,

- OR -

Have faces on your feet?

64

Poop your pants every time you answer the phone,

- OR -

Pee yourself every time someone says your name?

WOULD YOU RATHER...

65 Shower with a sponge that is covered with hair,

- OR -

Use a bar of soap that is covered with hair?

66 Be stuck in your room with 500 grasshoppers,

- OR -

Have the rest of your house filled with 5,000 cockroaches?

WOULD YOU RATHER...

67 Have farts so powerful that they make you fly,

- OR -

Burbs so powerful that they teleport you to other places?

68 Use a kitty litter box every time you need the bathroom,

- OR -

Always feel like you need to pee even after you have gone to the bathroom?

WOULD YOU RATHER...

69

Stick your hands into
a bowl of brains,

- OR -

A bowl of eyeballs?

70

Rub ketchup all over your body,

- OR -

Mayonnaise all over your body?

WOULD YOU RATHER...

71

Rather have eight legs like a spider,

- OR -

Eight arms like an octopus?

72

Have the bottoms of your shoes made of chewing gum,

- OR -

Have chewing gum stuck in your hair?

WOULD YOU RATHER...

73

Sleep with a bunch of skunks,

- OR -

In a pigsty?

74

Be chased by 100 moths,

- OR -

Be stuck in a room with 100 lizards?

WOULD YOU RATHER...

75

have a piece of food stuck in your teeth for the rest of your life,

- OR -

have a booger stuck in your nose for the rest of your life?

76

Walk barefoot through a field of cow poop

- OR -

A hallway filled with slime?

WOULD YOU RATHER...

77 Have to use a phone that fell into a dirty toilet bowl for the whole day,

- OR -

Pick a phone out of a dirty toilet bowl once?

78 Change a baby's dirty diaper once a day,

- OR -

Smell a dirty diaper every time you see a baby?

WOULD YOU RATHER...

79

Wear your friend's old underwear,

- OR -

Use their old toothbrush?

80

Wear wet socks,

- OR -

Wet gloves for an entire day?

WOULD YOU RATHER...

81 Wear underwear made of poison ivy,

- OR -

Underwear dipped in maple syrup?

82 Smell a grandpa's armpit,

- OR -

Smell a baby's butt?

WOULD YOU RATHER...

83

Have a pet llama that spits at you,

- OR -

A pet pig that smells really bad?

84

Grow a tail,

- OR -

Grow a pig snout every time someone called your name?

WOULD YOU RATHER...

85

Suck your sibling's toe,

- OR -

Chew on their toenails?

86

Lick the bottom of your shoe,

- OR -

Wear a pair of dirty socks as gloves for the whole day?

WOULD YOU RATHER...

87

Be chased by a swarm
of bees,

- OR -

By ten skunks?

88

Use leaves as toilet paper,

- OR -

Wash your hands with mud
whenever you go to the
bathroom?

WOULD YOU RATHER...

89

Have a stranger blow
their nose into your shirt,

- OR -

Have your friend sneeze
in your face?

90

Eat a worm,

- OR -

Let it crawl around your
mouth for an hour?

WOULD YOU RATHER...

91

Have ants crawling all over you,

- OR -

Have lice in your hair?

92

Walk around with a wedgie the whole day,

- OR -

Shave off all your hair?

WOULD YOU RATHER...

93

Not shower for a month,

- OR -

Or wear the same clothes for a month (including underwear)?

94

Swim in a pool filled with sardines,

- OR -

Filled with milk that has gone sour?

WOULD YOU RATHER...

95

Drool whenever you see food,

- OR -

Cry every time you see an animal?

96

Have a baby throw up on you,

- OR -

Change a baby's dirty diaper?

WOULD YOU RATHER...

97

Lick a tot seat,

- OR -

Lick a shower floor?

98

Sniff your dog's butt,

- OR -

Eat its food for a whole day?

WOULD YOU RATHER...

99

Be trapped in a world made of boogers,

- OR -

One made of earwax?

100

Be super hairy,

- OR -

Super smelly?

WOULD YOU RATHER...

101

Live in a dirty trash can,

- OR -

Have trash cans as feet?

102

Smell like a skunk,

- OR -

Look like a skunk?

WOULD YOU RATHER...

103

Eat a spider sandwich,

- OR -

Have spiders crawling all over you?

104

Swim in a pool filled with green sludge that tastes delicious,

- OR -

In a pool filled with chocolate sauce that tastes like slime?

WOULD YOU RATHER...

105

Clip your friend's toenails,

- OR -

Or have them put their feet in your face?

106

Pick your nose every time someone says your name,

- OR -

Fart whenever you see someone you know?

WOULD YOU RATHER...

107

Walk barefoot through a hallway filled with sewer water,

- OR -

Smell sewer water wherever you go?

108

Drink a bottle of rotten milk,

- OR -

Sweat rotten milk?

WOULD YOU RATHER...

109

Lick the pavement,

- OR -

Lick the bottom of your shoe?

110

Step in dog poop,

- OR -

Find dog poop in your bag?

WOULD YOU RATHER...

111 Walk barefoot for a whole month and never wash your feet,

- OR -

Wear the same underwear for a week?

112 Have all of your food taste like old cheese,

- OR -

Smell like old cheese?

WOULD YOU RATHER...

113

Have toes for fingers,

- OR -

Have a toe stuck to your face?

114

Have to sniff your dog's butt

- OR -

Have everything smell like your dog's butt?

WOULD YOU RATHER...

115

Lick your dog's face,

- OR -

Eat dog food?

116

Lick a turkey's feet,

- OR -

Have your feet replaced with turkey feet?

WOULD YOU RATHER...

117

Have the world's sweatiest back,

- OR -

The world's drooliest mouth?

118

Eat spaghetti and hairballs,

- OR -

Noodles and toenail clippings?

WOULD YOU RATHER...

119

Kiss a frog,

- OR -

Eat frog legs?

120

Chew on your parent's toenails,

- OR -

Wake up and not have any toenails?

WOULD YOU RATHER...

121

Live on a planet where everything smells like dog poop,

- OR -

A planet where everyone greets you by making you hold dog poop?

122

Run into a wall of manure,

- OR -

Slippy slide into a pool filled with other people's sweat?

WOULD YOU RATHER...

123

Eat your boogers,

- OR -

Drink your sweat?

124

Fart uncontrollably whenever you laugh,

- OR -

Fart loudly whenever you walk into a room?

WOULD YOU RATHER...

125

Eat a rotten egg sandwich,

- OR -

A rotten meat burger?

126

Have really smelly feet,

- OR -

Your breath smell like feet?

WOULD YOU RATHER...

127

Brush your teeth with mud,

- OR -

Rub mud all over your body?

128

Never brush your teeth again,

- OR -

Never have a bath again?

WOULD YOU RATHER...

129

Clean your friend's toilet

- OR -

Never go to a clean toilet again?

130

Wear someone else's stinky shoes for a whole week

- OR -

walk around the whole week with shoes on your hands?

WOULD YOU RATHER...

131

Wear a diaper the whole day,

- OR -

Pee uncontrollably the whole day?

132

Eat cat food,

- OR -

Eat five whole limes, including the skin?

WOULD YOU RATHER...

133 Scrub the floor with a toothbrush and then use it to brush your teeth,

- OR -

Use a cloth to wipe your whole house down and then use it to bath?

134 Have an invisible submarine

- OR -

An invisible magic carpet?

WOULD YOU RATHER...

135

Not be allowed to wash your hands for a week,

- OR -

Not be allowed to brush your teeth for a week?

136

Run through a bed of mashed potatoes,

- OR -

Swim through a pool of honey?

WOULD YOU RATHER...

137

Have to eat every gross thing you set your eyes on,

- OR -

Only eat rotten eggs for a week?

138

Grow a new nose every time you sneeze,

- OR -

Another tongue whenever you cough?

WOULD YOU RATHER...

139

Slip and fall into
a tub of slime,

- OR -

Have slime fall from the sky
whenever you walk outside?

140

Never wear shoes again,

- OR -

Never wear underwear again?

WOULD YOU RATHER...

141

Have eyeballs at the tip of each finger,

- OR -

Have them on each toe?

142

Pee your pants,

- OR -

Let your dog pee on your leg?

WOULD YOU RATHER...

143

Smell like tuna fish for the rest of your life,

- OR -

Eat nothing but tuna fish for the rest of your life?

144

Step in a pile of horse poop,

- OR -

Smell horse poop wherever you go?

WOULD YOU RATHER...

145

Sleep in a bed made from mashed potatoes,

- OR -

One that is made from boiled eggs?

146

Eat egg salad for the next week,

- OR -

Drink lemon juice the whole week?

WOULD YOU RATHER...

147

Grow a camel hump
on your back,

- OR -

Have a chameleon tongue?

148

Eat the diet of a pig,

- OR -

The diet of a cow?

WOULD YOU RATHER...

149

Lick your friend's scab,

- OR -

Pop your friend's pimple?

150

Have your friend pee
in your pool,

- OR -

You pee in your
friend's pool?

WOULD YOU RATHER...

151

Have your pants disappear randomly throughout the day,

- OR -

Start growing lots of hair on random parts of your body?

152

Eat your dog's diet,

- OR -

Eat your cat's diet?

WOULD YOU RATHER...

153

Lick the subway station floor,

- OR -

Lay in a pile of manure
for a day?

154

Grow fingers on your elbows,

- OR -

Eyeballs on your elbows?

WOULD YOU RATHER...

155

Work at a garbage dump
for the summer,

- OR -

Work in the sewers for
the summer?

156

Leak green slime from
your nose,

- OR -

Pink slime from your ears?

WOULD YOU RATHER...

157

Eat nothing but pickles
for the whole day,

- OR -

Pickle-flavored ice cream
for the whole day?

158

Grow moose horns from
your head,

- OR -

Swap out your legs for
octopus tentacles?

WOULD YOU RATHER...

159

Live on a planet where everything smells like dirty socks,

- OR -

On a planet where everything is made out of dirty socks but smells nice?

160

Eat a raw onion at every meal,

- OR -

Not be able to taste any of your favorite foods?

WOULD YOU RATHER...

161

Let your friend sneeze on your hands,

- OR -

Eat a rotten egg?

162

Live in the sewer

- OR -

Live on another planet made off brussel sprouts?

WOULD YOU RATHER...

163

Have your brother or sister pick the foods you will eat for the rest of your life,

- OR -

Eat moldy cheese at every meal?

164

Be locked in a room filled with skunks

- OR -

Have the rest of your house filled with spiders?

WOULD YOU RATHER...

165

Walk through a pimple forest

- OR -

An eyeball island?

166

Drink a cough medicine flavored milkshake

- OR -

Eat cabbage flavored ice cream?

WOULD YOU RATHER...

167

Throw up whenever someone says your name,

- OR -

Have uncontrollable diarrhea for a week?

168 Clean out a cat box with your bare hands,

- OR -

Step in dog poop with your bare feet?

WOULD YOU RATHER...

169

Eat food straight out
of a dumpster,

- OR -

Eat roadkill?

170

Have a big bucket of snot,

- OR -

A big bucket of spit
dropped on your head?

WOULD YOU RATHER...

171

Rub other people's ear wax all over your skin,

- OR -

Have to taste the earwax?

172 Swim in a pool of 1,000 people's toenail clippings,

- OR -

Have it rain toenail clippings for a week?

WOULD YOU RATHER...

173

Never be able to get rid of the trash in your house,

- OR -

Eat from dirty dishes for a week?

174

Never be able to flush your toilet,

- OR -

Have to clean 1000 people's toilets?

WOULD YOU RATHER...

175

Diarrhea and not be able to go to use the toilet at your house,

- OR -

Have someone else have diarrhea and use your toilet?

176 Clean your neighbor's toilet for a year,

- OR -

Go to the bathroom outside for a year?

WOULD YOU RATHER...

177

Smell a stranger's stinky feet,

- OR -

Smell your best friend's farts?

178

Find a dead fly,

- OR -

A stranger's hair in every meal you eat for a week?

WOULD YOU RATHER...

179

Eat a dead fly pasta,

- OR -

A maggot pizza?

180

Lick the toilet seat at school,

- OR -

Have the whole school see you in your underwear?

WOULD YOU RATHER...

181

Have centipedes for arms,

- OR -

Have the body of a snake?

182

Have fungus growing out of your toes,

- OR -

Have everything you eat to look like a fungus?

WOULD YOU RATHER...

183 Chew a piece of gum that you found under a table,

- OR -

Have chewing gum stuck in your hair?

184 Fart really loudly but have no smell,

- OR -

Make silent farts that smell horrible?

WOULD YOU RATHER...

185

Be covered in snails,

- OR -

cockroaches?

186

Clean out a nest of spiders from the attic,

- OR -

Or a nest of rats in the basement?

WOULD YOU RATHER...

187

Have a pile of dirty diapers fall onto your head,

- OR -

Fall into a vat of rotten food?

188

Swim in a pool that lots of people have peed in,

- OR -

In a pool that has poop floating on top of it?

WOULD YOU RATHER...

189

Wear clothes that have been soaked in someone else's sweat,

- OR -

sweat uncontrollably for the entire day?

190

Eat a rotten apple,

- OR -

A rotten banana?

WOULD YOU RATHER...

191

Rub dog food all over your body,

- OR -

Eat it for every meal for an entire day?

192

Eat nothing but broccoli for a whole week,

- OR -

Have broccoli growing out of your skin every time you eat your favorite food?

WOULD YOU RATHER...

193 Have feet growing out of your head

- OR -

Arms growing out of your back?

194 Fart really loudly every time you try to whisper,

- OR -

Start sweating uncontrollably every time you answer a question?

WOULD YOU RATHER...

195

Be trapped in a room with 1,000 spiders,

- OR -

Have to eat ten spiders?

196

Have all of your teeth fall out,

- OR -

All of your hair fall out?

WOULD YOU RATHER...

197

Have a splinter stuck in your finger the entire day,

- OR -

Chew on tree bark for half an hour?

198

March through a pile of garbage,

- OR -

Jump into a pool of mud?

WOULD YOU RATHER...

199

Eat the diet of a rat,

- OR -

The diet of a cat?

200

Have hair for fingernails,

- OR -

Fingernails for hair?

FINAL WORDS

Thank you so much for taking the time to read my book!

I hope you enjoyed going through these gross "would you rather" questions as much as I enjoyed writing them.

But you should know that they have not finished yet.

See, you have this book forever. This means that you can share them with your friends and family again and again.

So why not head back to the start and get laughing all over again?

CPSIA information can be obtained
at www.ICGtesting.com
Printed in the USA
LVHW021215011220
672994LV00010B/161

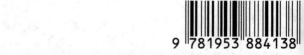